ANCHOR
BOOKS

THROUGH A POET'S EYES

Edited by

Steve Twelvetree

First published in Great Britain in 2004 by
ANCHOR BOOKS
Remus House,
Coltsfoot Drive,
Peterborough, PE2 9JX
Telephone (01733) 898102

SB ISBN 1 84418 336 X

FOREWORD

Anchor Books is a small press, established in 1992, with the aim of promoting readable poetry to as wide an audience as possible.

We hope to establish an outlet for writers of poetry who may have struggled to see their work in print.

The poems presented here have been selected from many entries, and as always editing proved to be a difficult task.

I trust this selection will delight and please the authors and all those who enjoy reading poetry.

Steve Twelvetree
Editor

CONTENTS

POUNDING

Perhaps pounding from Bristol to Hull,
- was her last day stressful - or quite dull?
Why did the great monster slow,
those thousands of years ago
and leave behind a woolly mammoth skull?

The weather must have become too hot
to wear that thick woolly coat she'd got.
Did she see a red mist,
fall with tusks in a twist,
never able to rise up from that spot?

Or were early men hunting her kind
and she was one the herd left behind
when she stumbled and fell
after the Arctic spell -
her skull to become a scientist's find.

With head in a museum somewhere,
likeness drawn in cave or secret lair,
prove you were seen by men,
pursued in their dreams then -
so - mammoth - does your ghost still
pound elsewhere?

Chris Creedon

LATE TRAIN

It's a cliché we could've expected:
our bubble burst by your overdue train.
The dregs of a four year conversation
The aftertaste of pretend champagne.

Your fingers cradled the cold remains
of the station's paperback tea.
Your eyes looked past reflections, stains,
the final stains of your sympathy.

Did it seem to you that I had moved
when, late, you moved away?
I joined the cut-outs of those once loved
who fade when they choose to stay.

I pictured you, watched by your reflection,
then taxi-counted on the grim parade:
The holidayed-out waiting re-collection,
their shorts showing tans about to fade.

I didn't feel your fingers clinging
To my face as our lives shook free.
My thoughts were a phone left ringing
for someone not where they're supposed to be.

Alex Fox

MOTHER'S DAY

A mother is a person very precious indeed
She gives you your life and helps you succeed,
She's there alongside you every step of the way
And urges you on when she thinks you might stray.

Her words of wisdom and advice are free
She gives you her time unstintingly,
She never asks for anything in return
Only that her love you will never spurn.

There's no other love as unselfish as this
To her your well being makes her life bliss,
She's your rod and your staff all rolled into one
Steadfast, reliable, someone to lean on.

It costs you nothing for one day in the year
To pay a small tribute to one you hold dear,
God gave you your mother thank him everyday
Because she's very special in every way.

J M Ward

WINDOW

I've always felt safe this side of the glass
It's okay for me, it's a different class
Don't feel no pressure in my little den,
It's good to be indoors again.
My room is my friend, it will never offend
Hear all I say, through night and day.

Had to go out, had a bill to pay
Took a lot of doing, my head was a ruin
The real world's with me, not that mess out there
Nightmarish vision, why should I care?
My TV's my window on what's going on
Don't need their help to help me along.

When I'm outside they all step aside
I know I'm cool, it's them that's the fool.
They stare and whisper, it's always the same
I can play this lot at their own game.
Ain't dumb I know it, I'm really rather good,
When you're like I am, you get misunderstood.

It's great to be the greatest, always been that way
My window keeps me going, on what to do, what to say
Can argue with my telly, even smash in on the floor
But must have my window, like I must have my door.

I'm safe here with me, it's so easy to see
Life's a breeze, I feel really free.
Don't need anyone, just me, myself and me,
And my friends are my room, window and TV.

So why am I feeling so edgy today?
Itching to be out there, wanting to play.
Can't say I've felt like this before
Could change things completely, if I got out that door.
Can I do it? No, I don't think I can
I'll say it again, I'm safer where I am.

The feeling's still with me, but I'm screaming and shouting
Was really looking forward to having an outing
The room's a wreck, what have I done?
Nose against the window, I'm shaking with a gun.
This'll make 'em like me, this'll make 'em come
Blood and glass all over,
Did I miss out on the fun?

Fred Brett

THE ORCHESTRA

The violins said to the orchestra, 'We really don't need you,
We can do it all ourselves for we are quite a few.'
The cello said, 'You need our help for where would be the bass?
You are high and fiddly, you really have no case.'
The double bass joined the fray, 'Without me you've no ground,
I anchor the whole orchestra, I'm the best thing around.'
The flute and piccolo started up in high quivering voices,
We always have the melody, we are the people's choices.'
The oboe, clarinet, bassoon put in a plea to be heard,
'We give colour and texture,' they quickly observed.
The brass said quite strongly, 'When the music needs to be loud,
We come in with our mighty power and the audience is wowed.'
The drum took up the argument and banged away with strength,
'I keep the rhythm going, I can play at great length.'
The triangle joined in next with its tinkling note,
'I can be heard above everyone, with my shiny, silver coat.'
The castanets and maracas each had their say in turn,
'We are effective for colour, of that everyone should learn.'
The xylophone clattered out its thoughts, as its hammers struck
the keys,
'I am suited to fast music and do all I can to please.'

Mr Sopranino, the conductor, came and tapped his baton on the stand,
When there was total silence, he started them with his hand.
Gone was all the squabbling and saying, 'I'm the best!'
For they all played together, even down to the rests.
The music they were playing was a lively symphony.
The whole was made of every part joined together in unity.
And so it is with people, its not the individual part
But working all together and doing it from the heart!

Rita Hardiman

SEARCHING

Searching
For the meaning of life.
Searching
Through all the trouble and strife.
Searching
For something I cannot find.
Searching
For some peace of mind.
Searching
For love, happiness or is it wealth.
Searching
For the best of health.
Searching
What am I searching for?
Searching
Will I search for evermore.
Searching
For I know not what
Searching
For something I have not got.

Shirley Stanford

LOST

I am as a ship
Without a rudder
Wandering without
Direction now that
You are no longer
Here with me
Dark and desolate
Of mood as
The raging sea
Without direction
I turn and twist
Dreaming of your
Sweet face in
Another place
I am as a ship
Without a rudder
Wandering without
Direction now
That you are
No longer here with me.

Penny Kirby

A FIRST

I've got a grandson
As cute as can be
A first for me
To dote upon.

However many they'll be
They'll be love for sure
To hope to inflate
If more or not be.

To share the joy of infancy
Admiring innocency
Praying for the unknown
And all responsible.

Influenced wholesomely
To nurture and flourish
On love and meekness
Through trying times.

Oh if more of energy
Or any other need
What superb beings
We think we be!

Be whate'er we are
In thankfulness
Correcting all we can,
To ever be true
To whomever we be
Before God especially.

Rachel Taylor

BYE

I lost my heart, along the way,
A crowded room, another day.
People talk, no one listens,
Bye

Please don't try to talk me round,
On my path, I am bound.
What's it worth?
Bye

I can't see, beyond the trees,
This tortured wood, is on its knees.
Death is near.
Bye

Darkness comes, to us all,
I can't see, beyond my fall.
What can I do?
Bye

Mike Curran

HOMO SAPIENS

Homo Sapiens sagacious species
despoil globe into minute pieces.
'Freedom for all' is cardinal claim
start a war and land reclaim.

Some serene lands, devoid of soil
are procured by cartels, who drill for oil
they begrime the world in useless slime
to remain on earth till end of time.

Galactic travel is millennium dream
demanding energies and dollars supreme
suggest we defer this project proud
as world is becoming a needless shroud.

Alex Branthwaite

WOOF

You are my pal, you are my friend
'walkies, walkies' a lot of time we spend
Walking the country, walking the town
Walking up, walking down
Happy days strolling with my dog
Down the pub and in the fog
So happy with kids such a gentle Labrador
It's almost as if you know the score,
'Good boy Penfold' as you bark at the post
We walk along the Pembrokeshire coast
You wag your tail, I buy some chips
I eat some fish, you lick your lips
Such fine memories of my canine chum
In the van with my mum
A faithful friend when I needed benevolence
To my Labbie dog I give reverence

Richard Appleyard

PARADISE BAY FOR A MEMORABLE STAY

We're back in Malta once again, so hard to keep away,
It's programmed in us to return; another special stay.
The staff are there to greet us at our favourite hotel,
For catering is what they do, and do it very well!

The Merill restaurant feeds us up with meals that satisfy.
Maltese desserts are such a treat for everyone to try.
Just taste the wine, join in the fun, it's holiday in style
You won't remember times like this for many a long while.

Our days get filled with water sports, but best are Monday nights,
As Kris and Lawrence fill the hall with musical delights!
Such sparkling sounds from Maestro Kris, while Lawrence plays
and sings.
Old limbs get moving on the floor, like angels without wings.

Just for a moment we forget about the tapping feet,
We might be in a concert hall, such music is a treat!
So thank you for your music Kris - the highlight of our stay.
It's well worth all the travelling to come and hear you play!

It's hard to single people out, for all just play their part,
Ensuring that our Malta friends remain within our heart.
Before we leave we'll give a plug to duty staff at night.
Joe rules OK at the front desk, CCTV in sight!

If you will have us, we'll be back again next year it's true,
It draws us, we can't keep away; the friends, the sea, that view!
Nigel and Gillie send their thanks to all you special crew,
We'll tell our friends to visit you, they're bound to like it too!

Gillian Humphries

Do Unto Others . . .

We all need somebody beside us
to share in the things that we do
to pick us up whenever we're down
and make us smile when we're sad and blue.
We know that we all need attention
a cuddle, a cosy, a kiss
for these little tokens are so special to give
yet for some, so easy to miss.
The love of another is precious
to be special to the one that you love
and to devote your life to each other
both on Earth and in Heaven above.
So when you find your somebody special
hold them close and don't ever stray
and never forget to show them you care
or someone else just might take them away.

Dawn R McPherson

MAY

Heavy cloths are put away,
the sun has come this bright May day.
Nature such a splendid thing,
brings the birds to chirp and sing.
Blossom fades, a tiny breeze,
scented lilac fills the trees.
Bees awake from winter's sleep,
yellow flowers smile and peep.
Soft white clouds go floating by,
April showers wave goodbye.
Drinks are poured to blur the mind,
thoughts then turn to summertime.

Tom Clarke

NEW WORLD

I see that all the fields are gone grazing animals too,
there are streets, houses, flats and offices in their place
no farms or countryside as we once knew.
Only parks exist to go to.
The streets are full of litter.
Vermin runs by your feet.
Crime is just a way of life, murder in the street.

Jean Bailey

TIN BIRDS

I'm glad tin birds can fly if you don't dream you die
And I was dreaming that I was caught smuggling dreams into Malaysia
For which the penalty is death
But they perched a tin bird on a clothes line
And they said if this bird don't fly you die
And it flew like a swallow
I'm glad tin birds can fly

Oh for a dream that is sweet and nice
Of a chocolate lady skating on ice
A marzipan warrior
In martial array
Sweeps her up in his arms and takes her away
To a land far away near the peppermint woods
To a castle of liquorice and allsorts of fudge
And they fall in love and live happily ever after
And have lots of children in mint condition
Sweet dreams

Philip Corbishley

THE ROYAL

The Royal William hotel overlooking the river
how quiet and beautiful it was to look through the
window at the swans swimming by,
how beautiful and serene they looked,
looking so proud,
with their long necks held up high.
We'd have a few drinks, then stroll by the river
to feast our eyes on the beautiful land
throwing bread to the swans from our hand,
The cathedral in the background looked divine
maybe one day my lover and I would marry there
in June when the weather is fine.

M J Chadwick

THE HOUSE

Bless this house, its roof of thatch,
the timber sides which don't quite match.
From rising damp, I beg of thee,
and woodworm warping, keep it free.
Bless the entry, fashioned so
that visitors may come and go
without restriction. Bless the ground,
the wooden decking all around.
When winter winds blow, strong and hard
I do beseech you, be its guard,
retaining in an upright mode
our pretty miniature abode.
Bless all those who eat within
and keep them healthy, far from thin.
Lord if it please you, heed these words,
preserve this house to feed the birds.

Valerie Calvert

MOTHER'S LOVE

No one gives you love like your mother,
You should love and cherish her,
Mothers love to be around forever,
Never asking for anything in return,
Then they are taken without question,
Please rest in peace my dear mother.

Jackie Jones-Cahill

SINKING OF THE SHEFFIELD

Toll for the Sheffield now under the sea
went 8000 miles to set the Falklands free
A missile from the Argentines
went through her stern
Within a few seconds, she started to burn

The Captain and his gallant men
fought the blaze like mad
When they saw how hopeless it was
they left, feeling very sad

Bereft of life beneath the sea
lying on her side
When the people of Sheffield think of her
they think of her with pride

She was built as a fighting ship
and she proved it on that day
The men that perished on her decks
in our churches, for them we pray

I feel sorry for the ones that are left
the mothers and the wives
When the Sheffield was sunk that day
the love one's gave their lives.

                                         R I P

Bert Booley

FOR YOU KAREN

I would climb the highest wall for you,
I would get the birds to sing for you.
Get the sun to stay out for you,
I would do anything for you.

Steven Borysewicz

LIVING IN DREAMS

Longing to be there in the middle of that life once more,
We were agile then, leaping from place to place, living life to its core.
Imbibing all the sights, the smells, as our excitement burns,
Holding hands, walking through a forest of trees and ferns.
Loving, thinking our youth would last, our energy, our zest,
Forgetting that as time goes rushing past, this time will be our best.
And so we go on living in our wonderland of years long past,
Knowing deep in our hearts of course, that only dreams can last.

Marj Busby

MEDICAL BARRIERS

I rang for an appointment the other day
'Is it an emergency?' she barked, to my dismay!
That iron lady of the doctor's reception
Trained for the people, by the Gods of Deception

Her check-point staffed by high-heeled feet
General Protectors of the medical elite
Aware of all the boils on bums
The acne infested, the swollen tums.

In order to pierce her routine rhetoric
I profess that I am gravely sick
Then she asks (as if she had the right)
My severity of pain, my medical plight.

Then I relate, I need a doctor's call
A request she doesn't like at all.
'Give me your address,' she adds with some disdain
'Forget it!' I say, I'll bear the pain.

Ian Bowen

RECIPE FOR A MONSTER
(Be prepared to run when the recipes finished)

Dragon paws,
Demon claws,
Mix and stir with fear.
Monkey tails,
Lizard scales,
Throw in a lion's ear.
Shake the mix,
Add Pixie tricks,
Or maybe a fairy's tear.
Then add some weeds,
An ogre's tweeds,
Completion's almost near.
So finish off -
With a pickled sloth
And then get out of here.

Jay Berkowitz

WISHES

Wishes really can come true,
Maybe not the way we want them to,
But in a sort of round about way
Things come good at the end of the day.
You may wish for a kiss from someone you love,
Or just hold their hand or give them a hug.
You may just get a friendly hello,
But that is better than nothing, you know.
Sat looking at embers all aglow,
Watching memories replaying, oh so slow.
If you had your life to live again,
Would you take the same path
Though filled with pain?
Or would you cut out the bad and the sad
And be left with the happiness you thought you had?
Tears of joy can come from tears of pain
And start to live life over again.
But until our wishes all come true,
There's not so much that we can do.

Ellen Chambers

THE SAMURAI

A whisper on the wind, the sun's soft light,
The flutter of banners left and right
The snorting of mans' noble beast
Unseating riders from the East.
Senses fading, sight and sound
Blade sunk deep within the ground.
Once, twice, thrice, he rises strong
But sinks once more to the baying throng.
Head hung low but spirit high
With upturned eyes, prepares to die.
Metal and wood and feather of goose
Fly as one, they are let loose.
Out of the sun they descend like rain
To inflict their wicked, deadly pain.
Never a cry, he knows not how
Eyes glaze over, head doth bow.
With one last breath, he tries to rise
Breaking shafts before their eyes.
Frozen in motion, life ebbs away
Ending his struggle this fateful day.

Paul Lawrence

THE SCARLET ROSE ON THE SEVENTH BEND

Tommy was walking with his sweetheart
Down the road which had seven bends
Rambling roses mingled together
And among the hedges were little wrens

He plucked a rose very carefully
And placed it on his Jenny's hair
A fragrant soft, scarlet rose
For this girl, so young and fair

The sun was shining brightly
As they walked there, hand in hand
They gave each other a little smile
As they drew closer to the sand

The beach looked so exciting
With white waves among the blue
They paddled their feet together
And splashed each other too

Love was in Tommy's eyes that day
He loved Jenny with all his heart
No one in this whole, wide world
Would ever tear them apart

They lay as the sun was shining
Wrapped in a loving embrace
Two young lovers, just starting out
As they kissed each other's face

The sun descended slowly
As they walked the seventh bend
They didn't see the headlights
And their lives came to an end

So if you're walking to that shore
Observe the seventh bend
A scarlet rose forever blooms
And its fragrance never ends

Geraldine McMullan Doherty

PEOPLE HURT

The tears that fell have long gone,
The beat of the drums that I felt in my heart,
The memories that were and now overturned pages,
The thoughts are like the rivers that flow,
They come, they go and only I know.
People hurt, people cry and we always ask why,
People walk, people run and have all the fun,
Sometimes, we do not stop to think who will hurt,
Some will go to all extremes and flirt.
Remember if you want to know,
To hurt that person will always show.
People dream of everlasting love,
To reincarnate and become a white dove,
To fly high in the skies above,
And to remain for ever in love,
People do not want to take the blame,
They are scared of being ashamed,
However, if people hurt they ask themselves why,
Why or why, did I?

Maggie Hickinbotham

THE RACING PIGEON

A dot on the horizon
zooming your way in,
Five hundred miles away
that's how far you've been.

My heart, it is a-beating
like a Kettle drum
The adrenaline is flowing
all because you've come.

A superior species
to navigate your way
Over fields, hills and seas
to get home on the day.

You really are amazing
to find your way alone,
However far I send you
you fly your way back home.

Your wings are shutting down
heading for the nest
I'd better clock you in
so we can beat the rest.

Tina Scott

IF I HAD THREE WISHES

I remember reading 'Sinbad' and 'Aladdin And His Lamp',
When I was still at school and just a lad.
Their daring deeds excited me I wished I could be them,
Especially for the wishes that they had.

Their genies were both stuck inside an old lamp and a bottle,
So to be freed, they promised wishes three.
I've often wondered what I'd do if somehow I was granted
Three chances to change something - so let's see.

I think the first thing I would wish for is to end all wars -
It seems the pain and killings never cease.
The tragedy of every war since time itself began,
Is no one wins - there may as well be peace.

And there's something else that's been around since man
first trod this Earth -
Disease has claimed the lives of countless folk,
But greed and avarice have seen us concentrate on profit,
What's spent on saving lives is one, huge joke.

My third wish is that no one on this Earth should ever hunger,
When thousands have more than they'll ever need,
They still want more, but waste so much that they
could give to others,
They just won't recognise their arrant greed.

My final wish! (If I may presume, I know I asked for three!)
But this one's most important, in my view -
It's that the power who made us all, who guides us every day,
Ensures my first three wishes all come true.

Geoffrey Leech

CAN YOU?

Can you see the colours in a rainbow
Or feel the summer sun upon your face?
Can you smell the fragrance of the flowers
Or run like other people, in a race?

Can you hear the wind up in the treetops
Or taste the sweetness in a chocolate bar?
Can you laugh when someone tells a funny story
Or cry when you see a falling star?

Can you reach out and touch the one who loves you
Or is the pain too much for you to bear?
Can you forgive what's been done to you
Or those who only want to stand and stare?

Can you believe that he could let this happen
Or will you not apportion any blame?
Can time heal all the pain and suffering
And take you toward that eternal flame?

William C J Iddon

POLITICAL CORRECTNESS RULES OK

When Bush came to Britain last year
He said, 'I have nothing to fear
For your freedom of speech
Is granted to each,
So your protests I'm willing to hear.'

Alas, what he'd failed to note,
As he made that much-quotable quote,
Was the limits now laid
On what can be said -
Or the PC brigade's at your throat.

You can criticise middle-class whites
But not blacks - that infringing their rights.
Muslims are taboo
As is Hindu and Jew
But a Christian's fair game for your slights.

Though some mullahs spit hatred and lies
Inciting the faithful to rise
And preaching Jihad
We can't say that they're bad
Instead we must all sympathise.

Osama can murder your kin
But you can't throw your keys in a bin
Whilst cursing his face,
Or the whole Arab race
Will demand a large part of your skin.

Now the Thought Police stand at your side
If you broadcast your views, far and wide.
Thus poor Kilroy-Silk
And those of his ilk
Must be gagged, though the truth's on their side.

Anne Wild

PLENTY MORE FISH IN THE SEA

Oh dear cod, please kelp me
for I am full of trout,
everything seems out of plaice
for she had changed her tuna.
All it seemed, was a load of haddock
we'd always seem to roe,
then she left at prawn
the best girl I could ever crab.
It just didn't seem to whelk
now it seems I've lobster.
Does she know how I eel?
she kept her feelings squid,
it's late at night, it's so shark
I wonder what she's dolphin?
Will she come back, please clam!
but - it's not that shrimple.
It's not a piece of fish cake
it just don't seem pike,
seems she's gone far, far a whale
and she said that I was a starfish.

Dean Paul Riches

A GRANDAD'S CHAIR

They take me for granted, they don't care,
I'm an old, forgotten Grandad's chair.
I am hardly used and rarely cleaned
Though once I was and once I gleamed.
I stand alone in a corner dark,
The dust being all that leaves a mark.
Am I so ugly in this new age
Who was once golden, now faded beige?
I may be withered and not too strong
And I might not even last so long.
But take an interest, I'm still yours,
I've stood aloft during two World Wars.
Respect my age, I still provide
A friendly comfort to rest or hide.
So when you see me, don't run, don't stare,
Make me a remembered Grandad's chair.

Tim Horwood

MORTAL BLOW

And such a mortal blow to lose heart's faith -
Choking in the rivers of its blood.
The red walls torn by pain -
The red walls torn as no other could.
And torn again, yet struggling on -
Through days and nights alike, symmetrical
Lines of torture, with freedom in sight.
Invisible thread that binds you tight -
Tight toward your own demise.
Until on weakening breath those uttered words -
And you're alone, what you craved for, but
Have never known.
Rather the bruises to hide, but appear in unity -
Than the reality become the opposite.
Now free, but still a prisoner to yourself -
Still a prisoner to their words, forever scarred inside and out.
And feeling such a mortal blow -
More painful now,
Because you know.

Philip Naylor

HEART ON A SLEEVE

Every time,
I build a wall,
To cupid's arrow,
it shall fall.

And every time,
I feel the skin,
I feel the wall,
collapse within.

When lovers see
the love so bright,
Their frightened hearts
flee from its sight.

To leave still burning
a love unfulfilled,
And once again
a wall to rebuild.

Sid 'de' Knees

LET DOWN

'Carrots' they called me when I first went to school
Like an orange spike, my hair stood up as a rule.
I'd freckles that sat on the end of my nose
And I'd boots that laced up which covered my toes.

My eyes were brown and my lashes were thick
But my skin was dead white, which made me look sick.
I saw Lucy one day for the very first time
She'd eyes of blue and fair curls and I wished she were mine.

I was eight, she was ten
But given a chance, I'd have married her then.
Unfortunately she took no notice of me
She whispered and giggled and laughed with glee.

I bought her a dolly, but she pushed it away
I got fed up and played football the rest of the day.
I'm not going to bother about any more girls
Especially those with silly fair curls.
I'll stick to boys' games and have a ride on my bike
Cos those are the things that I *really* like.

Jacqueline Bartlett

SOCRATES

Praised from
on top of the
mountains
or brought
down to your
knees.
One person's
version of the
events
and the other's Socrates.

Philip Allen

SHOW ME

Show me a garden
where love blossoms through
the earth full of riches
where sweet roses grew
that once held a magic
a secret within
to open my heart
up to many a thing

Show me a meadow
so wild and so free
where beautiful flowers
surrounded me
and all that I dreamt of
for many a day
no longer seemed so far away

Show me a valley
where harmony waits
and happiness follows
when I open the gate
hills of distinction
with shades of green
the most beautiful land
I have ever seen

Show me a forest
of whispering trees
with all of life's answers
wrapped up in the leaves
memories resurface
I've held deep inside
as I look to the future
with a sense of pride

H Berry

A Voice With No Name

*(Dedicated to our soldiers who are in Iraq
and their parents who live their lives with them)*

in despair and turmoil this day began
we follow the news and the radio we scan
we are the parents of a soldier a son that we lent
our love child our son our soldier was sent

gone off to war in freedom for Iraq
this soldier they sent the son we want back
no letters are coming no phone calls to home
we are parents of a soldier and we stand here alone

there is no one to tell us where our son is today
we can't look to the future we just wait and we pray
two soldiers are missing some British have fallen
we are frantic with worry and no one is calling

we pick up the phone and a soldier we hear
'i'll check on your son please try not to fear
your son is now safe' the soldier then said
'for twenty-four hours so go back to bed'

the voice with no name is the person we thank
no face for this soldier a corporal in rank
he gave us both hope and a day off from fright
he's the voice of our future we pray for at night

Dianne Audrey Daniels

COLD AS STONE

Is life worth living without love?
Where your heart has gone cold as stone
Never giving your all for fear of loss
Knowing that you'll always be alone

The inside may look very warm from without
But it's cold 'cause the affection is lost
It's cold on the inside, as only we can know
No one allowed close, that's the cost

People come and go in our lives
Memories are in your heart to stay
We change, move on and survive
Only true love lasts till your dying day

We dream impossible dreams
It was just a thought that I had loved
Not able to give me what I need
One day they'll come like an angel above

And then I'll be able to know
That warm feeling, a tender glow
Dreams unlocked, your heart overflows
Love melting all that's cold as stone

David McDonald

FLYING FISH

Another day our boat cuts through the water
Thought-provoking days are gone,
Materialising once more, favourable sea conditions
So our minds don't wander too long,
Predominant the winds as though we row in the sky
A day of prospering influence as flying fish pass by.

Resilience, great courage hinders all humility
Pioneers sporting blistering hands,
Jacked up on adrenaline declarations of divine favour
Synchronising breathing, this gruelling slog demands,
Westerly surface currents and trade winds set us free
Mental limits push us far, fair winds and following seas.

Fiona Ben-Dror

A RAINY DAY

Rain, rain, does it never go away?
That is the thought I had today.
I know they say it does the gardens good
but surely not to leave big puddles right where I stood.

The place was flooded - couldn't see the grass,
in the middle of the lawn stood a duck, as bold as brass,
it just poured and poured down throughout the day,
the times I got wet I just couldn't say.

Now I am home where it's dry and cosy
wasn't long before my cheeks were all rosy,
tomorrow may be cold and perhaps no rain,
that will be good as I run for my train.

Oh for the holidays to come around again,
lovely hot sunshine - we hope - instead of the rain,
springtime is only round the corner, people say,
then the daffs will be out, and we will thank the rainy day.

So perhaps the rain is not so bad after all
when we talk of the flowers growing so tall,
when I am inside, where it is dry, looking out,
I wonder really what I am moaning about.

Carol Anne Crompton

A Plea

Spite so vile, a temper in shreds,
Vicious his manner, his schemes are bred.
With the snap of dignity, comes the anger and shame.
Selfish and ignorant is the blood in his veins,
Denying obtusely the finger of blame.
An outburst of lunacy will brand him insane.

His tyranny reigned, his fists obeyed,
His tongue razor-sharp administered pain.
Began one day commenced his rage,
A character formed but never to alter;
So found its anarchy at this young age.
And from that day set out a boy,
Whose habit and aim in its desperate ploy,
Would bully and scar, intent to destroy.

His lovers were many, all seeming so weak,
Controlled by his games, his whims and his will,
They stayed and they suffered greatly until;
One day while sad, injured and sore,
They snapped to their senses and vowed no more!
Endured all they had, they could not bear to take,
Another blow from him with their lives at stake.

So courage they mustered, got brave and broke free,
From the man they once loved, at last they would see.
Necessity of strength to get up and leave,
To safety from his clutches, again able to breathe.

But one would remain for all of her days,
Accepting his brutality and manipulative ways.
A woman so feeble with similar mind
Would stay to witness her abuser's decline.
In love's fair name she would stand fast at his side

Defending his actions with bruises to hide,
His errors excused, behaviour forgiven,
She awaits the next time his fury is driven.
Her innocent children, they see all and hear
They listen and sob as they live in fear
Fresh little lives in bitter distress
Deserve a better chance, than domestic mess.

So, to the woman I address, you know who you are;
It may appear far or completely amiss
But strength is within, I promise you this.
Be brave and do right,
Begin the end of the lifelong fight.
Endeavour to make two thousand and four,
Count for your peace and so much more.

K L Jordan

THE VISIT

In this lonely wooded copse so dark
My terrier gives a tiny tentative bark
As if to say, hey there's something there
Come sniff and see, if you dare.

A dense black shape from in the shade
Of elder looms large, it appears man-made.
A big black sightless eye seems solemnly to stare
Of a damp and dank neglected smell I am aware.

Now Jack, he rushes in with glee
To find some foes or maybe just to see.
Whilst I am cautious, quiet and reverent
My senses heightened, my actions pent.

I feel that souls around me wake and speak
And urge me, step into their domain so bleak.
So through the tangle of creeper and sharp thorn
I push and tear a route into this home forlorn.

The roof has gone, save the rafters bare
And there's a broken rotting wheel-back chair.
Where once did sit a mother, babe at arms
While her husband toiled hard on neighbouring farms.

The walls are wet and green with moss and dripping fronds
And ferns grow tall in corners where the ivy bonds.
I hear the wind moan in the ash trees overhead
It's like the sighing of the residents long dead.

In the other tiny room I hear Jack scratch and whine
He's staring up at a shelf of stained, warped pine.
Where a tired old kettle holds a noisy little brood
Of baby robins calling their mum for constant food.

And as I stand with Jack at heel, we hear a flutter near
So proud the feathered mother returns and shows no fear.
So once again this old house protects its family inside
I give my blessings, grasp his collar and turn aside.

I fancy as I glance back into the growing gloom
I see a wave from where the sweet briar bloom
I hear a faint high voice call out to me and Jack
Come again some day to visit, please come back.

Jean Selmes

WELCOMING THE NEW YEAR

As the old year fades away and we look forward to the new
We think of friends and relations both far and near
We remember great events that enriched our lives
And our own personal sorrows and joys of the past year

We consider what we did and what we might have done
Could we have done better? Did we try hard enough?
Some times were joyously easy and life was sweet
But there were times that were painful and oh so tough

With the new year beckoning we see that life is a blank canvas
Whether we tread with care or forward excitedly leap
The future is unknown to all but a gifted few
We reminisce of good times and memories forever keep

With hope we enter the new year with our heads held high
The old year is already the past and part of our history
Forward, the only way fate will allow us to go
Taking one step at a time we continue our life's story

Teejay

WIMBLEDON

It's that time of year, the tennis is here,
a time for strawberries and cream,
the players come out and start up their match,
a grand slam win is a dream.

The courts are green, the sky is blue,
the umpire's sat in his chair,
it's hard to get tickets, they sell so fast,
but one year I'd love to be there.

When the players come out,
the crowd comes alive,
there are claps and cheers and shouts,
there's Tim and Greg battling it out,
but it's Agassi who makes my heart melt.

I remember when Agassi won the cup
on a Sunday in '92,
I was really pleased to see him win,
after all the hard work he did do.

With aces and volleys and lobs through the air,
and ball calls, a good and bad batch,
at the end of the day, the umpire will say,
'Well done, that's game, set and match'.

Rachael Ford

A BINDING OBSERVATION

Frogs jump on tresses in seaside towns and never hit the shore
Certain beings kick themselves never to be restored
Freaks do ponder certain dwellings of the mind they miss
Other sorts laugh out loud and sort of jeer and hiss
Flagrant are those who follow themselves as God but aren't the same
Muddy is the blood of the truly damned with only themselves to blame.

John Ebeling

TIME

Time goes by so quickly
Now I am getting old,
I often wonder why this is
It's a puzzle never solved.

I plan to do so very much
In each and every day,
Somehow my plans go haywire
Why is this the way?

I look back on my school days
They seem to never end,
Wished every minute to whiz by
Couldn't wait for the weekend.

I only wished I hadn't wished
For time to go so fast,
When I was young I did not see
Every minute should last and last.

But that is life no matter what
We may do or say,
Must make the very most of it
Enjoy every minute of each day.

J Naylor

WINTERING

I'm forcing my way through winter
by the pinprick of a cold moon
eyeing me with contempt for my warm blood
escaping in gasps of fog, born
from a raw, grey day. It drips on the tiles
and through the holes between once warm warrens.

I'm forcing my naked breast to feel the chill
of another night-morning drumming
to the swill of pint-guzzling puddles
and bubbling drains of sick water from sodden fields.

A new mind set? Square shoulders, chin in
cutting the wind, positioning the rain cold, cold,
facing the frost or fire of men as if of no account.
All for the sake of form and self-respect.

Diane Burrow

To Sarah

Oh wonderful,
my heart beats like a
thunderblast.
Oh wonderful
as I gaze
at thee
in all thy
radiant beauty.
Oh wonderful,
thy bright orbs
shine divinely
oh so finely.
Oh wonderful,
our love without
the need of lust.
Oh wonderful
and the Lord
glances down
from Heaven's
serene crown.
Our saviour is
oh wonderful.

David A Bray

FLAMES OF LOVE

Love has charmed and enchanted many,
Evading minds and dreams.
It strikes without rhyme or reason,
Nothing else matters it seems.
Our love is a powerful love,
It's so magic, yet so real.
We keep each other steady,
And on an even keel.
You're my personal shaft of sunlight,
And I your summer rose.
Hand in hand for eternity,
The flames of love will forever burn.

Donna Salisbury

THE ROSE - QUEEN OF OUR HEARTS

I'm the flowers' queen,
I have a sturdy stem,
Prickly thorns and leaves so green,
I grow in an earthen bed near a fence,
I love the humidity that's so intense,
I love the showers that fall on my face,
I live in this wonderful garden,
It's such a peaceful place,
By midsummer I'm in full bloom,
I grow tall so that I have much more room,
To dance and sway in each warm sunny day,
I love the days that are so breezy,
Sometimes I love to take it easy,
I feel so lazy in the days,
That are so warm and hazy,
My petals I open and close,
I love to elegantly pose,
Everyone's praises I really love to hear,
I really love spring and summer,
They're the best seasons of the year,
My sweet nectar is enjoyed by the bumblebee,
I look round and see,
So many colourful flowers,
That all keep me company,
All these things mean so much to me,
Autumn is looming,
No more am I blooming,
No more do I have scent so sweet,
No more am I basking in the summer's heat,
Summer slowly begins to unwind,
No more are my petals soft, silky and refined,
Now I can feel the winter's frostbite,
No more are my petals oh so white.

Joanna Maria John

GOODBYE BRITISH VALUES

Unless we start to care,
our country will be lost, the damage done is way beyond compare.

Our history is trampled into dust,
was it really worthwhile just to teach the female how to lust?

Deep down in Yellowstone, the Earths began to groan,
the magma rising slowly, ticking off time we have to moan.

What a shame the great men of the past,
could not instil in us their virtues that did last.

The end will soon begin,
what good will be designer wear without you to fit in?

Had we just used our brains,
we would not be close to the ape mixing with his remains.

Both liqueur and those pills,
plus smoking dope has took away their wills.

All strikes will be a rout,
as there will be nothing left to fight about.

So let the Pope in Rome say us a mass,
where once was Great Britannia there is now a nationwide
dark underclass.

Jean Paisley

DEDICATED TO THE ONE I LOVE

The first words I spoke to you
Were words of love and hate.
Love to hate you, hate to love you,
Hold me, hug me - suffocate.

You are monstrous, vile, hideous,
Repulsive to my all-seeing eyes.
Dragging your own acid red coffin
Spewing your murderous cries.

I watch as you creep towards me,
As you slither, slither on by.
Blood pours through my soul
When you uncoil by my side in a death-cry.

'I love you,' I scream, 'I love you.'
Does that pierce your emotion-proof shell?
And when you throw me into that pit,
I swear I shall put you through Hell.

You forced me into this murderous deed
And you laugh, laugh, laugh when I cry.
Come closer, snake, come closer now
Watch, watch our baby die.

Morney Wilson

YOUR FRIENDSHIP

Your unswerving friendship, a priceless gift,
worth more to me than any cash or gold,
has often given me a timely lift
when I've felt my morale about to fold.
Do I deserve this love, this shining light
to gently guide me when I lose my way
and to illuminate the darkest night,
leading me to another, brighter day?
The beauty of your soul has sustained me,
like food and drink give sustenance to you.
From dark depression you have set me free,
set my spirits soaring with hopes anew.
Hold onto my wings, let's fly together,
sharing love and happiness forever.

Clive E Oseman

NO FINAL END

The world goes round and life goes on,
In your heart the memories do bond.
There is no way to say goodbye,
That remains in spirit, way up high.
Nothing dies, this is no end,
A place is prepared for us to lend.
Just live your life to the full,
Enjoy yourself, be good to all.
Here on earth you will remain,
There's much to do, don't throw it away.
Do not feel or have any fear,
Your loved one's not far, but very near.
There is a purpose on this Earth,
A test of time, from beginning of birth.
Be glad to have this gift of life,
Sons and daughters, husband or wife.
We are God's creation till death do us part,
With light in our eyes and love in our hearts.

Mary E Gill

ISOLATION

Turn out the light
Close the door
Put nil by mouth
Upon this door
Give him no sky
No birds that sing
No buds that burst
With joy in spring
No date, no time
To know the day
No shaft of light
To make his way
No stars, no moon
No air, no tune
No sun to warm
His heart of stone
Let him feel
The heartfelt pain
That brought the tears
Like winter's rain
Keep him in an empty cell
Where loneliness and silence dwell
Let him while away his time
Befitting this heinous crime

Janet Vessey

MY MUM

The one who gave me life, held my hand, walked by my side
Catered for my needs, my mentor and my guide.

Held me close when evening came, then to the Lord we'd say a prayer
She'd dress me up in pretty clothes, sit me down and do my hair

Made me melted cheese with milk, nicely toasted under the grill
And took us all on holiday, to places like Rhyl

On summer days we'd walk up to the park
You, my dad and my sister, all having a lark

One spring you had a baby and we a new playmate, a little brother
My sister and I watched as you nursed him, waiting for our turn
                                                to play 'Mother'

Now we're grown up and you have grandchildren to enjoy
They make you laugh and bring you joy

I couldn't wish for a better mother and no one could give more
These words were created within my heart for the mother I adore.

Jil Moorehead

HIP OPERATION

I am going into hospital to have a new hip
Yes, I'm glad to be rid of it; it's giving me gyp
Pains in the groin, and pains in the knee
Won't it be lovely? Soon I'll be free
I'll hop, skip and jump if the surgeon says fine
They're using my old hip to help a new line
Well there's all sorts of things an old hip can be used
I'm glad they can use it, not for refuse!
They're welcome to mine, yes, every last chip
I'll dance with the new one, well, just a wee bit
I may take a holiday, at least go on a trip
The things I can do when I'm back in style
Watch out all you people, Joan's running the mile
My other hip too, could use a replacement
I'll put down my name, or slip on the pavement
When the next hip is done, it will be time for knees
Please treat them gently; they're beginning to freeze

Joan Prentice

MIDNIGHT CALLER

There's a full moon tonight
The air is mysteriously rife
I lie; low for my prey
My hunger craves life

I thirst for you my sweet sin
As I'm addicted to your smell
Come a little closer
For an engagement with Hell

I sink in my teeth
As you crumble in my hands
Devouring your soul
Draining your glands

Bitter sweet nectar
It tastes so good
My gut is now saturated
With your toxic blood

Rachael Cowham

THE YEOMEN OF MOELFRE HILL

Three windmills stand there up on high
Waving their long arms down at me
Expressing perhaps their great relief
Now at last being allowed to run free

In face of the wind, almost soundless
They go about their important work
Generating power to feed the grid
A production that they will not shirk

They cost many thousands of pounds
But pay for themselves in three years
Let us hope this will provide some rope
To help allay some country folks' fears

That they are a blot on the landscape
Voicing environmental concerns
Opposed to these persistent producers
Of energy that the population yearns

So carry on with your gyrations
Grey wavers of electric field wands
Let the passage and the fullness of time
Reveal the true value of your fronds

Early mills spun their sails for food
Fulfilling a most valuable want
None more so than in Holland
Where many old mills are extant

But far outstripping those numbers
New mills provide electric power
To a nation lacking hydro-electric
Achieving far more with this tower

And so it can be in Great Britain
Where pylons went up for the grid
Enabling power stations to deliver
Electricity to all points in the bid

To bring progress and technology
To a country so often in the dark
Where gas and candles were the norm
Before the onset of the electric spark

V T Clements

UNTITLED

A candle
burning brightly,
in my midnight window.

Quiet,
behind the mirror,
of my windowpane.

Your gentle smile,
suffused in darkness.
Garlanded in space
by, the amber glow,
of early morning.

Slips, silently away
into the warmth
of sleep.

G Lysenko

THE LAST GOODBYE

Goodbye dear sister Mary, your life is past,
We loved you to the very last,
We'll not weep for you but courage take
And love each other for your sake.
Sweet memories of you will always remain,
Until one day, in paradise
We'll meet again.

S A Walker

SANTA'S GROTTO

There was a Santa's Grotto
Featured in the local store
Where the youngest of the family
Taken at the age of four

Then as Mother waited
He purposely strode in
Pulled off the reindeer's antlers
Causing quite a din

As Santa remonstrated
His beard was pulled aside
The gift sack also rifled
Which really hurt his pride

Santa then resorted
To little children's hearts
Only to be rewarded
With a kick to private parts

The establishment's detective
Asked Santa what was wrong?
But Santa's swift reply
Was worded rather strong

The police were duly summoned
Thinking Santa was at fault
Saying charges might even follow
With accusations of assault

As the constable made enquiries
A similar kick was then received
And from his police duties
He had to be retrieved

The inevitable outcome
The family banned from persons there
Santa refusing employment
In grottoes everywhere.

Robert Muir

Some Keys To Life

Friendship is the key with where to start
Truth is the key that puts trust in your heart
Knowledge has the key where foundations you find
But wisdom is the key for the enquiring mind

Honesty is the key where the policy is best
Peace is the key that takes care of the rest
Tolerance is the key with the patience in waiting
Compassion is the key that finds the reason

Happiness holds the key to the purpose we seek
Humility is the key that protects the meek
Forgiveness is the key where you find the need
Strength has the key with the power to succeed

Grace is the key in the balancing act
Diplomacy is the key that demonstrates tact
Health shows the key that is clearly in bloom
Harmony plucks the key that plays the tune

Communication is the key to the connecting door
Love has the key that takes you right to the core
Touch is the key with the senses that tell
Good health is the key in the wishing well

When trust holds the key and in faith there's no doubt
And belief is the key in what knowing's about
Life is a magical journey with all keys within reach
To unlock the power of potential in each . . .

S M Wilson

BUSY BEES

As busy as a bee
Seeking his goal
Busy as a collier
Digging his hole

The bee is so busy
And ever so keen
But a bee with a brain
Is the one called the Queen

The proud working collier
That lives like a mole
Lost all his pride
When they filled in the hole

Quantity not quality
They thought the best
Ignoring the miner
And his bad chest

Consider the warning
To all busy bees
The miner died young
For willing to please

Ioan Pearce

COURAGE

There are many kinds of courage
Shown in so many ways
But we cannot always find the path
In which our courage lays
There's times when courage fails us
And we cannot make a stand
And times when we must take
Our courage in both hands
It takes courage to be pleasant
When everything goes wrong
But you will find that somehow
Something will come along
Each day we need more courage
To help us on our way
And we need to save some courage
To fight another day
Through all the years of courage
And all the things we planned
We remember all the courage
That saved our dear England

Dorothy Cordier

WEEPING WILLOW

Weeping willow reaching down
To gently sweep across the ground,
As rays of sunlight fall between
A canopy of pale green.

Weeping willow there you are
Beneath the sun, beneath the stars
Whilst all around, the world may change,
My weeping willow's just the same.

Weeping willow back in time
Little hands and feet that climbed
Weeping willow through the years
Through the laughter and the tears.

Weeping willow older now
Weeping willow, broken bough
Where leaves in gentle breezes blew,
Now empty space, unwanted view.

Weeping willow do not fear
No need to weep, no need for tears
Weeping willow, big and strong
Still standing here where you belong.

And when the winter turns to spring
Weeping willow, you will bring
Your leaves of green; a canopy
For all around the land to see.

Suzanne Kaye

SILENT SEA

From blinded eyes a heartfelt plea,
To make these feelings a reality,
But in return a waveless sea,
A silence spoken just for me.

A thoughtless dream drifts on by,
Forever lost to a sunless sky,
A lifeless smile in reflected eye,
Powerless to question why.

Those hidden waves, that heartfelt plea,
Swept away, lost at sea,
Ever the tide to run free,
A beatless heart drums for me.

Unspoken words to tearless cry,
Still here motionless I lie,
A wakeless dawn ready to sigh,
Waiting for that sunlit sky.

Richard Ackrill

NO TIME TO THINK

Who told him to find someone who listens?
The trouble is nobody does that any more
They're preoccupied with lifestyle,
Status and fashion to the core,
Gimmicks, drinks, no time to think
Stolen thoughts and worse, ideas
With little understanding, of what they may imply
And never meant to be sincere.
If it was popular to be whipped
Who'd refuse leather and a cane?
Feeling confident at least in social worth
How could such a mortal mind refrain
From redundant forms of indulgent scorn
Heartfelt, in collective chatter?
Nearby fears once more endeared
Prejudice moves on to another chapter.
Next month's issue of Vogue more like
Trends move on like the wind
Without opportunity to judge these days
Diversity's a sin.
How can he state his own desires
Free from a modern clan or tribe
While he's required to hire a choir?
Is that why he's still a lowly scribe?

David Mason

CHERISH

Sometimes I sit here all alone and I feel an overwhelming love for you.
My mind reflects on past events, how I used to be, how I am today.
If only I could find the words to express how grateful I am to you.
Just a few lines perhaps, that would show you how much I care.

And I cherish every time you enter in my thoughts,
In the way I think and the way my mind flows.
The inspiration I get from you when my resources are low.
You enable me to take another step and choose the right way to go.

The mystery that surrounds you is such a wonderful thing.
It strengthens my inner self and causes my soul to sing.
A song that has no words to hear but the eye can surely see.
An inner glow you have given me that set my spirit free.

And I cherish every time you enter in my thoughts,
In the way I think and the way my mind flows.
The inspiration I get from you when my resources are low.
You enable me to take another step and choose the right way to go.

I am bound by your love and care for now and evermore.
Each day you make me feel so strong and much more self-assured.
To know each day that you are always here for me,
Has caused me to give my heart and soul to you completely.

And I will cherish every time you enter in my thoughts,
In the way I think and the way my mind flows.
The inspiration I get when resources are running low,
Has enabled me to hold my head high and choose the right way to go.

Valerie Anderson

THE END

The world is to be run by one giant computer,
Which will kill off the tradesman and morning commuter.
All of the banks shall merge into two,
Which fight for the custom of myself and you.

Cars have grid-locked every road in the town,
Too much pollution has turned our skies brown.
Where there was ozone, there's only a hole,
Serves us right for not giving Greenpeace a go.

Prices go up but nobody cares,
The lottery has made us all millionaires.
The government has folded and the Monarchy are dead,
Our lives are all run by celebrities instead.

Humans are dying and the end is close by,
We never did make living up in the sky.
Our only hope was to live on the moon,
But looks like Earth was meant for our tomb.

Please don't be scared, I'm just trying to say,
That your future is heading this way.
It's not a straight road and has many a bend,
But one of these turnings could signal the end.

Adam Priest

ASYLUM

Please listen to the story I'm about to tell to you
Then you can decide if any of it is true
For seven long years I have been locked inside this place
But I am very much younger than the look upon my face.
At five o'clock in the morning they get me out of bed
They strap me to a chair and fix wires to my head
Electric shock treatment is what they're giving me
They tell me that it's good for me and it's called therapy.
Then after breakfast it's time to walk around the yard
But there's no chance to escape when you're watched closely
                                                    by the guard
Then it's back inside where time is yours for a while
You can read a book or watch TV as long as you don't smile.
Now the day is over it's lock up time again
You see I've been put in here because they think that I'm insane
But if the truth be known I shouldn't be here at all
Now I spend my nights crawling up the wall.
I just can't see a way of getting out of here
I don't think I could stand it for another year.
Sleep is the only relief I get in this miserable life
I really miss my home, my children and my wife.
They have all been told I'm dead, which you know is not true
But I'm trapped inside this wicked place, what am I going to do?
Being inside here has taken its toll on me
I've lost my fight, my will to live, there's no hope that I can see
So as I sit here all alone the thing that's really sad
Is that after all this time maybe I have gone mad.

Paul Bowler

DEATH THE UNWANTED CALLER

Oh! Death you cruellest caller on the common man
Why do you come a-knocking at my home?
What harm have we done there?
We had no worldly care,
You turned the lock - but you had no right,
Just like a thief steals in the night
You cast your hand right then and there,
And left our lives in deep despair.
No hunger, thirst or thought have we,
Your cloak of darkness overshadows me.
There is no sunshine, no never again
And our tears they fall like pouring rain.
Oh! Death your name just tears me apart
For you always leave a broken heart
Yet Death when we come face to face
I cannot run, you'll win that race.
I'll fight you though, though I may not win
Shall I banish you? Please don't call again.

Tracey Ellison

MAN

I used to grow veg'tables, fruit hung on trees
I gathered my berries, ate honey from bees
There used to be cattle providing my meat
This planet was heaving with plenty to eat

I walked through the moorland and fished in the lakes
made sweet smelling bread and nice tasty cakes
And all from the woodland, my own house I built
My sheep gave me wool and I wore clothes of silk.

Back then this land was a haven for man
My land full of milk and of honey
My need to succeed was called purely greed
'cause I wanted to make pots of money.

I fed all my beasts with some chemical treats
to make them all grow even faster
You said that one day I would be forced to pay
for causing a massive disaster.

My animals died as everyone cried,
'Stop bringing them all to extinction!'
I thought I knew best and I slaughtered the rest
and I never bothered to listen.

On a warm summer's day I watched rabbits at play
I thought I would have such fun
As they bounded around, a deafening sound
as I shot everyone with my gun.

I ploughed up the forests until they were bare
You said that I shouldn't but I didn't care
I'm thirsty . . . I'm starving . . . I don't find it funny
But now I have learned that I can't eat my money.

Mia Petersen

A Poet's Tale

They say I'm quite a poet - that I really have a flair:
I must admit I often seem to pull rhymes from thin air!
Any theme; it seems to me, is food for thought and poetry.
There's so much to think on - the words begin to flow:
Poets are like artists; painting pictures as they go.
Although the verses don't need to rhyme; somehow,
they always do in mine!

I try to imagine other worlds: like ours, but not the same:
Perhaps where wars do not exist and love's not just a name!
Then my thoughts return to everyday: humdrum routine -
and bills to pay.
I sit at my computer and type on the monitor's screen,
Sometimes, it takes only minutes to fill the blank that's been,
Yet, occasionally; I must say, writer's block gets in the way!

I've entered some competitions - but so far: no success;
It's proving harder than you'd think; the judges to impress!
Another poem I must find, from creative words that fill my mind.
If I feel nostalgic, I can look back on my past:
At times, I write what I recall, to make the memories last!
We're older versions of who we were then, but still fair game
for the poet's pen.

You, too, can take up poetry and help put the world to rights:
The pen can be mightier than the sword; conjuring such delights!
Wonderful hours spent along the way, brightening up the dullest day.
So, have a go! Give verse a try! It's easier than you're thinking:
Writing poems can be fun; it's almost as simple as blinking!
Now's the beginning of the rest of your days: poetry can colour them in
so many ways!

Maureen Mace

TRAPPED

Trapped inside the darkened cage, I smelt the smoke -
I thought my imagination was playing awful tricks again,
I gasped for breath.
Extractor fans kicked in - the fire alarm screeched its warning,
I couldn't get out!
Panic set in - I reached for my asthma pump for relief -
It didn't work.
I heard the sound of heavy footsteps, the jangling keys, shouting
voices - but they hadn't come for me!
I wanted to scream, but nothing came out like before -
My chest tightened.
I wondered momentarily if it was my time to die -
It wasn't.
I went to the window; the smell from the room below came
pouring into my lungs - I prayed that someone would come to save me -
They didn't!
What happened to care and consideration for others?
What did I do to deserve this?
I hid myself in the bathroom and soaked my flannel -
I held it across my face and breathed in the moisture.
Perhaps I'd live another day to tell the story - God willing!
I returned to my bedroom - the extractor fan went off at last -
The smoke and flames had gone for now.
Would it ever happen again?
I pray it doesn't!

Alicia Jenkins

No Regrets!

I'll never see your face again
nor see your smile
nor hear your voice
nor feel your hands in mine
with words to reassure me

Those words shall I not forget
once said forever spoken
no changes shall I make
no regrets, no pledges, and yet
thoughts of you remain
shall you remember me the same.

S A Baylis

ANOTHER YEAR

Another New Year is on its way,
Snow and ice not to stay,
Joyful parties, past and gone.
Hopefully spring won't be long -
Snowdrops in abundance to appear,
Bringing smile and good cheer,
Birds giving territorial call,
A warning to one and all.
Sheep giving joyful bleat,
Watching lamb struggling to feet.
The horse a foal; the cow a calf;
Their gambolling makes you laugh.
Dogs and cats' litters on display,
Watchful eyes don't let them stray.
Nature is a wonderful thing,
All joys it does bring.
What more could we ask
To make these joys to last?
Where do we as humans stand
In troubled society land?
What sense can we give
For everyone all to live?
Will peace in this world come to stay
Or is greed to have its way?
Can we the people ask you in charge
Your ideas to enlarge?
May they be for peace,
This for all would be the least
Can we wait till death do us part,
Or just be blown apart?

Bob Sill

WE CRY AND NO ONE HEARS US

We cry and no one hears us.
We perish and no one cares.
This indifference to our plight kills us.
We ask only to live.
We beg only to survive.

Our young are slaughtered for their fur.
Skins torn from still warm, young bodies,
Merely to grace a lady's body.
We are alone in our grief.
Abandoned by mankind, our grief is profound.

Why us? What crime did we commit?
Is it a crime in this world, to exist?
Must we pay for man's greed and indifference with our lives?
We too feel pain, mourn the death of our young.
Will the world be a better place with our going?

There was once room for all.
The world was created with a place for everyone.
Then came man and with him our destruction.
Must we die in vain?
Will mankind never learn.

Valerie Borland

FORGOTTEN AT CHRISTMAS

The snow keeps falling,
As time passes by,
Waiting for Santa,
To fly down from the sky.

He fell down my chimney,
I fell back to sleep,
But really what I want to do is,
Have a little peep.

I awoke in the morning,
And went down the stairs,
To find under the tree,
Nothing, it was bare.

I thought to myself,
Has Santa forgotten me?
For all the other children were
Full of happiness and glee.

My eyes filled with tears,
As I thought to myself,
Has Santa forgotten me,
And put me on a high, dusty shelf.

Everything around me,
Began to disappear,
For now I could see,
It was all coming clear.

Maybe I've been naughty,
I should have been good,
A dark cloud came over me,
There where I stood.

I am caught in this world, some sort of dream,
But I know, dreams aren't always what they seem.

Rachel Walmsley (12)

MAGIC MOMENT

Perching upon my washing line,
You sing your song, and it's divine,
Alone in the sweet morning air,
I wish I had someone with whom to share,
This magic moment you have given me,
Now you are flying back to your tree.
But as it's just us two,
This moment is for me and you,
And if later on you return to spend some time with me,
I will share my lunch with you, but not my cup of tea,
But to thank you for your song, if you wish,
I will put some fresh water, in your dish.

Maureen Arnold

GAMES

Help me please I have nothing to say,
Your games I no longer want to play.
Sometimes it's clear what you want of me,
Who I am, what you want me to be.

I'm strong, I know but what of you?
I feel the power, but what can I do?
People think it's all quite plain,
I'll leave and never see you again.

But this is life, and believe me, I can't,
What I've done we can't easily part.
Then there are the choices we have to make,
The course of the path we have to take.

Come now my sweet hold my hand,
We can do this and make a stand.
Hold up your head for all to see,
And remember you mean the world to me.

Dawn Graham

ASYLUM SEEKER

I don't speak English proper, mate,
No need to on my rough estate;
A job is not the thing for me,
I like to watch daytime TV.
I'll never work to earn my cash,
The dole clothes me in Adidas;
If I go short from time to time,
I simply turn to petty crime.

On market day I stroll through town,
Draw dirty looks from all around,
Don't care that I may cause offence
Crashed out drunk on the park bench.
This easy life I'll not relent,
Funded by your government.
To whom, you ask, are you now talking?
The name is Clive, born and bred in Dorking.

Craig Parker

THE SUIT

The suit of clothes that make a man,
The suit supreme a cloak of dreams,
You're clean and smart and have a tan,
A tie that's brash and shoes that gleam.

A magic mantle worn with pride,
And viewed by all with high regard,
A suit with stripes and silk inside,
You're standing still as if on guard.

The younger men are looking smug,
A suit, a uniform, a glove,
The old and wise can cut a rug,
And walk the walk there in the groove.

The suit the measure of the man,
A sign of his authority,
An aura bright around him ran,
You could have asked him back for tea.

David M Walford

LIFE

Sometimes I sit and wonder why
Life is so cruel to you and I
It takes away the ones we love
And keeps them in some place 'above'.

Sometimes I sit and wonder how
Saddened souls are meant to grow
When all life brings to them is pain

How will they ever love again?

But there's a light around the corner
And it's shining just for you
This is the light of others love
For they are smiling down on you.

Jo Nilssen

No Defining Words . . .

No defining words, I just know,
No pre-packaged sentiment, there's just nothing left to show.
And all the stars are falling from the sky,
So how come you have to pass me by?
Only the residue of ashes linger from the fire that died out,
Slowly but surely all my memories are fading out.

Washed out and burned out, naiveté's wrapped up in ribbon,
Reminiscence a cheap substitute, anticipates an existence of in-denial.
Turns out coincidence bought us together.
Destiny divides our paths
Twist of fate and it's no longer at hand
Each and every footstep reminds us of each wrong terrain we stand.

No defining words, I just know,
No pre-packaged sentiment, there's just nothing left to show.
And all the stars are falling from the sky,
So how come you have to pass me by?

Bilkiss Bashir

HELLO NAN

Hello there Nan
I hope you are fine
Becky is doing all she can
To get good grades
Katie is trying to be good
And not get into any trouble
They both think of you
Each and every day
You never got the chance
To meet little Lily-Maé
She was born
And I held her oh so tight
Hoping one day
That I might
Have the chance
To show you her pretty smile
So that she could sit and play
On your knee
For just a little while
But you can't see her
Maybe just from afar
As often the children
Look up at the shiny star
And say there's our nan
Watching us from above
Sending us love from Heaven
Sending us all her love
And each and every day
She looks at us and gives a sigh
Our nan now loves us
At her home way up in the sky.

Tracey Marie

BITTER WEATHER

Snow covers
Morning spring
Snowdrops
Weary clouds
Bring dreams alive
Whistling wind sounds
Church bells ringing.

A Hattersley

LADY OF THE ISLE

She sends me dreams
Her thoughts are benevolent streams.
She sends her spirit at night
Brings me visions, shows me a light.

Sometimes m'lady enters my mind
But this intrusion is always kind.
She plants suggestions, I remember on waking
Things to ponder as dawn is breaking.

She dwells on an island across the sea
Where she wields great power, spreads tranquillity.
M'lady comforts, she does not control
She utters mysteries to my soul.

From a clifftop in a white tower
She sends new dreams every hour.
My body lies still, my mind flies to meet her
Our dreaming minds embrace as I greet her.

I became aware of ancient feelings
Rivers of coloured waters, places of healing.
A golden gateway which lies to the east
The paths of the sun, knowledge and peace.

M'lady brings me to remembrance
When I am with her, my thoughts are a dance.
She leads me to where all things are known
My forgetfulness is soon overthrown.

She sends me dreams
Her thoughts are benevolent streams.
I know I will never be the same again
Until the next time she calls my name.

Ian Bosker

THE TRINKET BOX

I have an antique trinket box
An heirloom gift to me
    It has a gemstone studded lid
    It has a golden key.

It stands upon a little ledge
Next to my single bed
    So I can see it at a glance
    If I so turn my head.

But one fine day, 'tis sad to say
It was no longer there
    Some silent thief had taken it
    My gift beyond compare.

I tried to fathom how or why
The loss it made me weep
    To think he entered in my room
    And stole while I'm asleep.

Some days went by and then relief
'Twas hard to comprehend
    A suspect had been lately stopped
    And kept to apprehend.

My trinket box was recognised
And from a hoard returned
    With advice as to future risk
    From lessons keenly learned.

Reg James

TRYING TIMES

A night on the tiles - hiking for miles
Telling rude jokes to inspire the smiles
A day at the races - hoping to win
Downing some lettuce to help you get slim
Swimming in pools - attending schools
Enjoying yourselves like simple fools
Exercise biking - rowing machines
Improving one's features with miracle creams
Going down potholes - climbing above
Challenging obstacles like many do love
Saving of face when one has been caught
Cheering up someone who is feeling distraught
Tightening nuts - screwing in screws
Telling of stories that are making the news
Poetry writing that others call prose
Observing secrets by keeping out nose
Helping another get out of a hole
Befriending the bereaved as they you console
Attending church to join in the psalms
Informing the 'lost' that Jesus them calms
Spending of fortunes on beautiful girls
Solving a problem as the reason unfurls
These are the little things that turn out to be big
When the ill-informed mortal thinks it infra dig
Rewarding happenings to cheer up the low
Kicking your car when it refuses to go
There is much to favour let that be understood
A little of what you fancy - *will*
                        do you some good!

Jon El Wright

MY MADNESS

Nerves ran through me like waves,
The Devil rears from the caves.
Frustration soars through my skin,
You devil release all my sins.
Anger chills my veins,
Confusion fills my brain.
Desire reaches my heart,
These feelings, the body chart.
Yearning is deep in the soul,
Feeling is what makes us whole.
Love is life's rich potion,
Life is love's deep ocean.

Marsha Leone

HAT-PINS

And who will note the strength of men,
The daily donging of Big Ben,
The governing and law of lives?
The bastions of England's wives!
Old ladies . . . with their hat-bands
Vouchsafe our fathers' guiding hands.

From whose dreaming church spires proud
In skies of blue, all good and loud,
Peel the several bells to matins
Old ladies with their hat-pins . . .
The bastions of England fair
Who pray for those who could not care.

Roger Mosedale

I HEARD

I heard a nightingale singing,
aloft the valley green,
in reminiscence of you,
with your smile like never seen,
the rainbow of illustrious grandeur,
which ensued the passing shower,
reminds me of the good days,
when you shone like a blossom flower.

I heard a voice amidst woodlands,
portraying a radiance bright,
I think it spoke of you,
the light amid my darkest night,
stand proud as trees in honour,
dreams fulfil 'neath tender moon,
to embrace even unto the morrow,
when the sun shall sing its tune.

I heard the breeze whisper,
like a harp unto mine ear,
so cool - yet, so gentle,
for all solemn to disappear,
such solace in abundance,
as I walk my blessed trail.
all grandeur now embrace me,
on hearing love's unifying tale.

Steve Kettlewell

FRIENDSHIP NEVER DIES

As tears fill my eyes,
the clouds fill the skies.
The wind blows through the air,
cutting into your beautiful, long hair.

We walk along laughing and joking,
remembering the good times, looking and thinking.
We look into the past,
look to the future and know our friendships will last.

The road to happiness is a journey,
it isn't a destination, it's important to remain happy.
This past year the happiness you've given me is amazing,
our flames of joy will carry on blazing.

As tears fill my eyes,
it's tears of joy, we are not saying our goodbyes.
'This is not the end,' everyone cries,
for the simple reason, true love and friendship never dies.

Dominic Ryan

GRANNY'S LULLABY

The old spinning wheel was Granny's
She loved to sit spinning all day
The woollies she knit from her spinning
Would be the envy of lassies today
She crooned as she sat at her spinning wheel
As I sat down to look at her spinning
I saw a wee tear in her eye
She was upset and I wondered why
As she sat in her chair with her knitting
I asked why that song made her cry
Grandpa sang it to her as a lassie
And she called it her own lullaby
Now Granny is no longer with us
But I still see that tear in her eye
When I knew that she was thinking of Grandpa
As he sang her that old lullaby
Now they hold hands and sing it together
In that place they call Heaven in the sky.

Eva Smith

DARKNESS

Darkness comes not only at night,
Looking out the windows, there's not much in sight.
The sky is black and the moon lit bright,
This time at night most people get a fright.

You don't take much notice, you go to bed,
Although maybe not all some people may tread.
Some people may say that it's the most peaceful time of the day,
When there's not many kids outside to play.

Time passes so quickly and you awake to face the day,
People off to work to bring in the pay.
As the day passes and you've had so much fun
Playing with friends or resting in the sun.

Thomas Jamieson

LIVE AND LET LIVE

Live and let live
The way our world should be
Freedom for you
Freedom for me
Freedom for all
Be you black
Be you white
Freedom for all
It's only right

Greeny 2004

THE SKY TELLS MANY STORIES

I nearly died and forth I went to the other side
From there I thought I may fly
With the aid of pretend wings
To lead up to the infinite sky
With the dove of the freedom above . . .

To leave the darkness behind
Where it belongs
Down there and beyond.

In the reflections from where I stood I tried to take off
The gentle rolling hills got smaller and smaller
I saw the bleakness, the dark, the grey in the pools of water
I prayed it would fade away as the changing tides roll on by.

It was part of my mind
I've got nothing to hide
Maybe with the gush of the spiritual wind
She could lift me up and go beyond
Far, far beyond . . .

Hang on my destiny is waiting . . .
Falling, falling away from the black hole
Into the next creation of dreams . . .
It really does seem not so far away . . .

Then

I love the truth and all she brings
As it is carried on the wind
It is not an illusion or a delusion
Just the sublime standing in line
Of discerning reality making its fortune
I hold it dear, Heaven is here
Completely crystal clear, my dear
There is no fear.

Darsha Rees

A Grave Yarn!

Such gems they are and I'm enslaved
to two canny feline queens;
who seldom ever do behave,
however good I've been!

I beg, I bribe, cajole, enchant -
make threats to curl their tails;
but they've fathomed these are falsehoods,
for it proves to no avail.

Now I've found a secret weapon,
a sort of fancy, funny fad -
'If you steal my dinner from my plate,
or if you're very bad.'

I gaze into cool cat green eyes,
(that bewitch, seduce and mesmerise)
with a calculating silent stare -

'I'll have you carbonised into diamonds -
to dangle from each ear!'

Later

Dear reader, if you're flushed with fear,
or feeling slightly sick -
you really needn't worry,
it failed to do the trick.

When I was home late yesterday
I heard one mog to other say -
'We'll have her whiskered, into fish flakes
to mash up in our dish!'

Anita Richards

How Sweet The Forest

Come away, come away the sparrow said
Fly little soul, fly
Sing tiny saplings, sing tender shoot
Grow oh grow play loudly Heaven's flute
Come away, come away the sweet robin sang
Hush no more earth's stillest hand
Shout little maidens shout so loud
Dream smallest atom, dream among the crowd
Coo, coo calls woodland pigeon, home is my tea
Coo, calls the pigeon, for surely you can see
Where silver streams run, tides ebb, heartaches
Are touched by rivers tender flow
Oh mend broken heart, bandage pains denial
Come sweetest angels, with midnight smile
Blistering winds, curl around fated nook
Blow nature's fury across, pastures brook
Where we live under, protective sacred tree
Flooding tides of emotion, they touch you and me
God's earth runs damp, beneath our union
                    Sweet darling maiden
                    Here beneath my weight
                    How I love thee, how I love thee
Here I bless your sweet love, beneath God's greenest tree.

Ann Hathaway

REPENTANCE

As I look back on my life, from my prison cell
As I wait for my exit call
And I wonder at whose bidding did I answer satin call
I have had time for reflection, I repent all
I have done
The door that I take from my prison
Leads only to my death
But if I turn aside at my going, there
Is still one road left?

I will ask my Lord and Saviour now
To take my last walk with me
As I go now on my journey
He will be hand in hand with me
We will walk through that door together
For He has promised, even me
All my sins forgiven
As He died loving me.

Gate Keeper

A PEN WILL BE MY GUN

He is me
Eamon John Healy is my name,
My only job is to write poetry
Because on this Earth
I want fame,
Roses are red, violets are blue,
I think this one's been done before,
So I'll lock the window
And close and bolt the door,
I know one day that I shall meet my fate,
I hope in my poetry me you'll not hate,
For in tomorrows
And the days yet to come,
I'll live again
And in war
A pen will be my gun,
The odds on my life are as yet uncounted
Poetry is music to my ears
Am I a ghost where no ghost has gone before,
Or just a poet
Knocking
On
A
Lowly door?

Eamon John Healy The Warrior Poet

FORWARD AND BACKWARDS

One day in May
in a field strewn with hay
we noticed a certain swelling to the ground, a hump,
a pregnant bump.
The thought of what this might deliver
gave us all a shiver.
With our shovels we began to dig
like pigs for truffles in the dirt.
It wasn't long before a clang rang out
and metal door was the shout.
Prising it open a room appeared
and some feared this was the work of the Devil.
Inside was a suit unlike any we had seen before.
Could it be armour ready for war
and was this King Arthur's grave?

Someone said, 'Put the armour on
and then let's be gone.'
The task fell to me to complete the task
and fasten my mask.
Every man, woman and child left that room; save for me.
Dressed like a Christmas turkey ready for the oven
they closed the door.
Lights flashed on and off
and strange grinding sounds caused me to feel nauseous.
Then again the door opened showing a landscape
that was the Kingdom of Hell,
fiery red with an awful smell.
Was I dead and this place to be my bed?
Leaving the room I had feelings of doom.
Extra! Extra!
Read all about it! 'Mars lander sends
Back photograph of alien in space suit'.

Vann Scytere

REVELATION

Who says you can't go back in time?
I did the other day.
My daughter gave me a gift,
A scrap of wattle in a spray.
Her smile rivalled those golden blossoms,
Her sweetness, their perfume,
As I saw myself thirty years back,
In a similar sunlit room.

The flowers I send my mother now
Are sophisticated, in a sheath.
But suddenly I know that she'd prefer
A bunch of wattle or pale pink heath.
Now I know the real meaning
Of a gift right from the heart.
It's not the gift, or the content,
It's when love is the major part.

It's so easy to make a phone call
And have the bouquet arrive on tap.
Though undeniably beautiful,
This gift still leaves a gap.
That personal touch is missing,
That impulsive gift of youth,
When we gave of ourselves so fully
In all innocence and truth.

Patricia Adele Draper

THE REVELLERS

Here at the butt-end of our earthly stay,
Our hope all fled, comes yet another wealth
of revellers, to crowd our final day
With risqué laughter at our imminent death,
With cries of raillery and fully determined
To smite us where we stand; no pity
For those who lost their way amid the din
Of a gloriously corrupt and infamous city;
As though to steal from us once more
Our transient day of fame, a drunken crowd
Of fakers and buffoons banging at our door,
Loud, boisterous and self-righteously proud
To praise a century gone back to seed
And me alone to rail at their fell deed.

Hunter James

ETERNAL LIFE

Facts of life on the table, learn anything from Mabel;
Guess who's coming to dinner? A guy known as Eternal Life:
Best of six nothing new in that: year ending our hero in charge;
Flocked to see - Eternal Life:
Block-busted, event charged with emotion;
As much as you can say in a sprinkling of dust;
Goodnight sweet Prince adieu Eternal Life.

S M Thompson

THAT MAN

Paris was lovely in spring
I met that man who wore no wedding ring
Just an ordinary working class man
Who was washing a soup pan
That look in his laughing, smouldering eyes
Sent shivers down my spine
We downed glass after glass of wine
Talking, talking all night
I slowly, sensuously fed him a Milk Tray
We made love to sexy music all day
It just felt so right
This time,
I planned on a very, very long stay.

June Coates

LIFE'S OWN GARDEN

It's the gift born of life
that is presented each day
to a world full of colour
where I'll continue to play
like a child still in awe
of the wonders around
spread to enlighten, inspire
a nature refound
one of simplistic leanings
enduced by easier moods
felt only after some tastings
of nature's own foods
that nourish in splendour
fragrance pastures anew
for sake of healing my garden
to make it fertile and do
what is duly required
with a heart for a hoe
that can tend all these wonders
meant to flower each show.

David Patterson

CHANGE

We don't have the winters now
that we had years ago,
when roads were impassable
trees and hedges covered in snow.

We suffer now from mist and frost
for just a month or two
and that is reflected in what is lost
as plant life is not renewed.

There is no time for them to rest
before they are forced to bloom
and in consequence they are not at their best
as summer before them looms.

It is one of many a prophesy
that the seasons will change
and plants now flower as one sees,
there is no limited season's range.

Many species will gradually disappear
as summer heat becomes more intense -
over the next few decades I fear.
To save them needs common-sense!

What chance does plant life have
when homeless roam the streets?
The government ignores these facts
as such truths they will not meet.

They waste money exploring the Universe
or waging a war over false claims,
which puts logic in reverse
with their misguided aims.

We don't have the winters now
that we had years ago,
but we still have thoughtless governments somehow
who just don't want to know.

D R Thomas

A GREAT INVENTION

There is something I have noticed
that I think I ought to mention,
the Earth keeps turning all the time;
it's such a great invention.

The rain may fall on your house,
as it may fall on mine,
but wouldn't it be dreadful
if the rain fell all the time?

Of course, that couldn't happen,
for the Earth is very wise,
and changes all the weather
by rotating in the skies.

It's such a great invention,
and such a clever plan.
I think I'll go to London
and tell the weather man.

Alex Anderson

IF WE COULD GO BACK IN TIME

I often wonder how our ancestors would react
to our modern way of life
if we were able to turn the clock back
to that world of manual strife.
Would people who lived in those very old days
believe there would be a man on the moon?
The laughter that would erupt from them (and they would say),
'The man's a fool, he will be in an asylum soon.'
To tell of things we have today, television, washing machines,
wireless, antibiotics, test-tube babies
I wonder what they would say?
What a difference our modern way of life
would have made to them.
To have a nice shower with beautiful scented soap,
life would have been a lot easier for everyone to cope.
Wonderful buildings were erected in many years gone by
I only wish our ancestors could see our modern homes
as we can see their architectural buildings
standing proud in the sky.

Jack Fallows

WHAT IT IS TO BE BRITISH (AS SEEN THROUGH THE EYES OF A COMPARATIVE NEWCOMER)

From the corner of my mind, emerges -
Someone who is kind - considerate too -

He or she is mostly understated.
Although an ego that's inflated -
Opinionated too! - Hard-working -

Of devotion, there is a 'manly' portion
Ready in a crisis to pay what the price is
In order to get resolution.

Generosity abounds, loyalty too.
I know how this sounds - but it is true.

I'm speaking here of the 'man in the street'.
Sir, I am honoured to have joined the ranks of you!

Mary Fitzpatrick-Jones

I'VE GOT TO HAVE A FAG!

I wake up in the morning, I've got to have a fag,
I'm sat here in my nightie, oh! how my boobs do sag,
I give a cough and splutter, my lungs they start to wheeze,
I take another drag and put my head between my knees.

My doctor prescribed me nicotine patches,
He said they would help do the trick,
I said, 'They are marvellous, when stuck across my lip.'
I've had acupuncture, they stuck it in my ear,
Now I'm down to 50 fags and 7 pints of beer,
Out in the garden, amidst a cloud of smoke,
Frogs were conversing, please stop or we might croak,
I wish I could stop smoking, the money I would save,
Instead, I've bought another 500 and a headstone for my grave.
Cough! Cough! Puff! Puff! Cough! Cough! Splutter!

Ivor Percival

THE BLIZZARDS BLOW

The blizzards blow
Winter's first snow
Wish on a star
Moon so far
Sky of blue
Include me too
Embers of fire
Temper and ire
Call on four winds
Spiral and grin
Heap up tall mountains
Smooth over seas
Wild are the ways
The spirit frees
Dancing madly
Drumming oddly
Breeze to the trees
Daylight flees
Black, black, glossed lake of black freeze
Sneeze, sneeze, sneeze
Earth
Disperse
World left behind
Close your eyes
Still you mind
And shamanise

V Jenkins

A HIDDEN BEAUTY

If everyone stopped to look for one minute
To admire the world and everything in it
They'd see many things often taken for granted
So beautifully pure in a world so enchanted
The old twisted branches of every tree
The bustling hives of the worked honeybee
The burnt rising sun of every morn
The spirited birds that sing out at dawn
The rivers and streams through deep valleys run
And lustrous waters from the glistening sun
Things that always appeared to be
But whose beauty we often fail to see
For its charm that comes with no disguise
Is only hidden to those who shut their eyes

Jennifer Austin

TREE STRUCK BY LIGHTNING

I look like a skeleton, claws bony and black.
Destroyed almost by a lightning attack.
I've stood on this field over fifty years
Now with this cruel storm it's left me in tears.
I look like a skeleton bony and black,
Upward stretching to the sky,
An eyesore to every human eye.
No more my beauty, my leaves are all torn
Destroyed by this summer storm.
The lightning and thunder came with terror so strong,
Stole my heart with its roaring song.
I'm doomed now,
My only use once more is for logs
To burn on an open fire
Where once more I will glow again
Enlightening my heart within my flame.

Kathleen Gilboy

CHILDHOOD MEMORIES

Can you remember your favourite toy
that got you excited and jumping for joy?
Was it a space-hopper, or Barbie and Ken
That enthralled you for hours, again and again?
Mine was a dolls' house, so finely handmade -
where the dolls were princesses and I was their maid.
A miniature mirror with gold gilted sides
hung over the fireplace, with spotlights beside,
and Rosebud lay back on an old rocking chair
in a white frilly petticoat, with long auburn hair.
And curled up beside her was Candy, a cat,
who I carefully combed on a soft, sheepskin mat.
Then asleep on the sofa was always the collie
tucked between ragdolls, Lavinia and Molly.
How I recall so well amusing myself -
re-arranging the furniture, dusting dolls on the shelf.
I'd colour in tissue and make paper flowers,
I had lots of patience, I played there for hours.
No batteries to charge, or plugs to connect,
unlike the train set, which was nearly wrecked.
My brother assembled and connected the track,
but never could start it, did not have the knack.
With wires and plugs all over the station,
his face said it all, with a look of frustration.
Then I'd wait for the crash, and hear the loud thud,
he'd stomp down the stairs, and say it was dud.
And in a bad mood he'd march off to the shed,
ride off on his bike, his cheeks cherry red.
How I remember it well, although all in the past,
these much treasured memories will linger and last.
Not much of your childhood, you leave far behind
as pictures stay vividly alive in your mind.

Alison Lambert

THE LASTING NIGHT

The day may fade, the sun may set
And darkness may come
Rolling in on your life
Like the fog off the sea
Slowly surrounding you, making you stumble
As you try to walk along the path you thought was right.

Now and then you may fall
As the night so dark
Will not allow a light to shine
No stars twinkle, no moon casts an eerie glow
To light your way as before.

The night seems to last, never a dawn coming
So you can see the wounds you suffer
Only the pain is all you know
As you stumble through the lasting night
Hoping you can stay on course
To reach the goal you had dreamt

Before the night had come, to darken your life
To hide you from the joys, only allowing you misery
That beats you down
To the point surrender seems sweet

But you cannot surrender
The night will fade. And a new dawn will break
With a new path for you to walk
And dreams to dream.

Oliver L T Waterer

DUNKIRK

The beaches of Dunkirk are never at rest
Soldiers who died were amongst the best
Letters were sent home
To wives, sons and daughters
They told of the trenches
And about all the slaughters
Some found it hard to carry
All the memories of the deaths
Knowing their husbands had died like the rest
We admire them every one
Never forgetting the ones that are gone
The colour of the poppies
Reminds us of all the blood that was shed
The black is to remember to honour the dead
Time will come when war is done
But that won't bring back our loved ones.

C Latimer

NOISE FREE

What is peace?
It's sat in my garden on a hot summer's day
The trees are still and the cat's at play.

What is peace?
It's walking along a golden beach,
No seagulls in sight, so not a screech.

What is peace?
It's entering God's house of prayer,
Leave behind your worries for someone cares.

What is peace?
It's sat in my own armchair,
No TV or radio on, the doorbell? You dare!

What is peace?
It's the still of the night,
I look at the stars, they twinkle so bright.

What is peace?
I lay down at the end of the day,
Say a prayer, close my eyes and drift away.

What is peace?
It is sleep, no bumps in the night,
And Teddy agrees that peace is all right!

Rachel Mary Mills

HEAVEN SENT

A star fell out of Heaven
And floated gently down to Earth,
It was the star of Love,
The one that gives us birth.

That little star from Heaven
Touched the hearts of Hazel and Guy
And soon they had a baby girl born
With eyes as blue as the sky.

Oh welcome little Lara,
You are from Heaven sent,
You have brought so much love with you,
Especially to your dear parents.

That little star will lead you
Along the path of life,
He will guard you and protect you
From any stress or strife.

I wish you health, I wish you wealth,
And success in all you do.
May your life be full of happiness,
This is my prayer for you.

Phyllis Ing

ITINERARY FOR MADRID

Hamps and Hannam on the trail to Madrid
From there they will travel to the port of El Cid
There they will meet friends from USA
Then back to Madrid and Hotel Carlton to stay
It's all systems go for Hannam and Hamps
Well known in the States as the travelling tramps
They travel by train and also by air
Whenever invited they will always be there
Yes, they have travelled the world
Have Hannam and Hamps
In some countries you may find
A Hamps Hannam stamp.

E L Hannam

ABORTION

After breaking holy laws
They try to justify their cause
Claiming that it's no sin
To kill the unborn child within
Murder's wrong, this we know
The Bible even tells us so
Even as a last resort
There's no excuse for to abort
The rules aren't up for negotiations
They were made for all creations.

Colin McBride

JOSHUA

There's a beastie in my garden
it's chasing after me
There's a beastie in my garden
whatever can it be?
There's a beastie in my garden
it makes a terrifying sound
There's a beastie in my garden
when daytime comes around
There's a beastie in my garden
it makes an awful noise
There's a beastie in my garden
it's my grandson and his toys!

Jean Taylor

CHOICES

Two roads lie before me
Each with a life at the end
The first is straight and simple
And waiting is my best friend.

The other is not so clear
But everyone likes a surprise
I'd like to walk each new turn
And see with brand new eyes.

My life was always simple
But I don't want to choose
Now I'm faced with choices
I've never been so confused.

So where do I go now?
Which road should I take?
Should I go and join my best friend
Or leave his heart to break?

Becca Smith

SUMMER EV'RY DAY

So many years ago when I
Was barely bigger than knee-high
The world was safe, the world was good
And we enjoyed as children should,
Wise only to life's matinee
    And it was summer ev'ry day.

In blissful ignorance we played,
Blind to man's evil, unafraid;
No dangers lurked, how joyously
We revelled in our liberty;
Cares were a million miles away
    For it was summer ev'ry day.

No serpents stalked our paradise,
No vain distractions could entice,
We lived no lie, no mean pretence
For we were blessed with innocence;
Utopia could not decay
    When it was summer ev'ry day.

How soon we lost our childhood ways
To life's incurable malaise;
It stripped us of our simpleness,
The flawless gifts which we possess;
What would men gain if only they
    Could feel that summer ev'ry day?

But now it isn't long ago,
This world's a place I do not know,
This world is dark, this world's defiled,
More hostile than when as I child
I lived to laugh and dance and play,
    And it was summer ev'ry day.

Hilary J Cairns

OUTSIDE

He lives on the outside, always alone
The guilt he feels, that he has to atone
Here he is living, while his best friend is dead
Why it couldn't have been him instead

This time bomb of youth - proving how cool
An imaginary Ferrari he drove like a fool
In the guise of a Fiesta that couldn't take the strain
It's a nightmare he'll live again and again

Roads that were wet in a light growing dim
He'll never understand this monumental sin
Was aware of no danger, didn't see that bend
that was the night his friend's life would end

Didn't see the sign - too busy talking
But this was the night that death was stalking
Boy racer chancing at reckless speed
A grim reaper unable to conceal his greed

For the rest of his life he'll hear his friend's cries
As he cradled the body and death closed his eyes
Numb with the pain as the ambulance arrives
Wishing, wishing that he'd never learnt how to drive

No words to excuse, only action to explain
He can never forgive for causing so much pain
Destined to live - it will remain with him always
Alone on the outside - that's where he stays.

Emma M Gascoyne

PALE BLUE EYES

Through the eyes
Of a child
My heart will smile
Into your eyes
When the sun
Sets in the sky
You know I smile
In your pale blue eyes.

Helen Owen

FORTY-FIVE, GOING ON SEVENTY-EIGHT

Music today just moans and groans
Nothing like them Strolling Bones.
More a sparrow than any red rooster
Give them an injection, they need a booster.
I think they're just in it for the cash,
Here today, gone in a Jumping Jack Flash.

Who said the girls today can sing?
There'll never be another old Rusty Bed Spring.
Do they earn a vast amount of wealth
Not knowing what to do with themselves?
Are they a disgrace to each of their fans,
One day they'll wed The Son of a Preacher Man.

Many songs they play today it rings a bell
Like we heard years ago by Hairy Smells.
No matter each day how I do try
They'll never get to say he is My Guy.
For every song that was an old'un,
For the others then Silence is Golden.

Colin Allsop

ORCHARDS PLUS TREES COVER

Our airforce played such a large part
Cover from view became Germans' art
Used knocked carriers as sniper posts
Plus mobile hay stacks was real boast
Often would attack from side or behind
Seventy in cow shed eighty yards away
Hidden by hedge and trees save so close
For a time wrought havoc half-track pose

Sent six-pounders up after damage done
Return alone after shower was far from fun
Walnuts on tree I just had to knock down
Lonely time as my mates no longer frown

Our major came up looked so surprised
The mistakes were so obvious realised
Too late the carriers which brought guns
So took the bodies on backward runs
This was part of the holiday said I had
When got back to England and was so glad
Only to pick pieces of steel out with a pin
Justice in Great Britain just no such thing.

John J Flint

THE CHILD

How could you claim that black was white,
And hope folk would believe you?
If someone told you day was night,
Would they manage to deceive you?
Would you believe that dark meant light?
Or weak was really strong?
Can you get crooks to do what's right
If they don't believe they're wrong?
You'll never change a wayward youth,
Who's grown up free and wild,
It's not their fault, and that's the truth,
You should have taught the child.

Matthew L Burns

A SPRING ADVENTURE 1931

It was an error of judgement -
though the thought was so well meant -
to take a boy just three years old
to that adventure film so bold:

The hero swung from tree to tree
using vines so conveniently
to drop via overhead traction
to spoil the villains' nasty action.

Tribes at each other's throats
chasing down river in flimsy boats,
spears at the ready for a fight,
blades all polished, shiny and bright.

Heroine tied up to a tree,
screaming a bit obviously,
as through the trees with ape-like yell
swung Tarzan, going it like Hell!

The chimps and elephants join in
to round off all that jungle din,
and start a stampede at great speed -
then Tarzan's calming influence heed.

To emulate my hero's thrill
I tried next day some bedsprings skill,
but, bouncing high caused me some woes -
I overshot and broke my nose.

So many years have passed by since
that re-profiling made me wince.
Surgery's a possibility -
but a straighter shape just wouldn't be *me!*

Jo Allen

MY ASPEN BEAUTY

My Aspen beauty
I pledged my troth
To do my duty
And make you my wife
Forever and a day
And all my life,
See above a shining star
To guide me where'er you are,
Your noble head,
To follow shadow wherever it led,
You are my staff,
My daily bread,
Your enchanting laugh,
Your snub nose,
Your Bold autograph,
The perfume of your clothes,
You are my daisy,
You are my rose,
And though with love you drive me crazy,
Take me to summer days,
So long ago, so hazy,
May I always walk in your ways,
My Aspen beauty.

Alan Pow

SWAY

My little ray of sunshine,
That makes me want to smile.
My ginger, fluffy hairball,
That makes my life worthwhile.
She sometimes makes me shout
At the naughty things she does,
But there's never a day that goes by
When she doesn't make me laugh.
The reason I love her the most,
Is because she knows when I'm feeling down.
She comes and sits beside me
And takes away my frown.
I love her too much to be normal,
But I don't care, I know she's mine,
She'll never hurt or leave me,
And never say goodbye.
She sleeps upon my pillow,
And sometimes on my chest,
She purrs all night in darkness,
But I don't care, she's just the best.
Cos when I'm feeling lonely,
She'll sit there on my lap,
She makes me want to smile,
She's my one and only cat.

Sheralee Hoskin-Goode

A LITTLE MORE CAREFUL
(Dedicated to Sue Nicholson)

I'll be a little more careful
when it comes to falling in love again,
when I was with you
you broke my heart
and caused me so much pain.

I've been a little more careful
since you've gone away,
you've tried to fool me
by saying that everything will be okay.

Maybe you should be a little more careful
not to break my heart ever again,
because if you do
I shall cause you so much pain.

Chris T Barber

BACK TO SPACE!

Solar system, solar system, what can I see?
I see an alien flying round above me.

Solar system, solar system, what does he look like?
He is big and green with shiny eyes.
He has no hair and comes in disguise.
He changes his appearance so we don't know where he is.
He could be in your classroom, or creeping in your bathroom,
So don't close your eyes or turn your back on him at all,
Because one day you could bump into him
And you won't see anyone at all.
He'll take you back to space and hide you in a creepy place -
And you won't see a single face!

Shannon Wilcox (8)

A DOG'S LIFE

Tess, my golden retriever, is full of cheer and goodwill,
She is so very playful, and never wants to be still.
I don't feel lonely when I have her around.
Sometimes it seems as if her paws don't touch the ground.
We go down memory lane together, just her and I,
Walking for miles and miles looking at the sea and the sky.

I throw her rubber ring a distance away,
Off she goes and has a good run, enjoying her play.
Tess will bring her toy back, lay it at my feet,
Waiting for me to throw it again, giving her a repeat.
I do this until I am tired, and feel I have had enough,
Then Tess has to give in, not being too gracious, she thinks
                                         this is tough.

Tess lies in front of the fire, she loves the heat,
It's the good life for her, she falls fast asleep.
When I am having a bit of supper, she comes over to me
Then she begs and begs, and puts her paw on my knee.
Out come her Good Boy chocolates, she eats them with delight,
The rest are put away for another night.

While lying on her back, she kicks her toys in the air,
If she gets too naughty, she is sent to the kitchen, to sit in her chair.
While on holiday we climb up hills and go down dales,
We trek and wander on for many miles.
Dear Tess is a sweet and good friend to me,
And she always will be.

Rosina Forward

THE PHANTOM GORILLA

Key in the lock,
After twelve by the clock,
Just a snack before bed,
Open the fridge for the cheese and onion spread,
Boil the kettle for a cup of coffee,
Finish off that sticky toffee.
Better had undress downstairs,
Leave clothes folded,
Shoes and socks in pairs.
Need to be quiet,
Watch out for the creaking step,
Fourth from the top,
I wish this dizziness would stop!
Better go and take a pee,
This toilet looks very small to me!

Light through window,
I wake up surprised,
What's all that shouting - am I being chastised?

'Door not locked! Kitchen, a disgrace!
Wardrobe used as a lavatory!
Clothes all over the place!'

I must disagree, it can't have been me!
I left it all neat,
I don't deserve to be in this plight,
It looks like we were burgled in the night!
Or could the legend of the phantom gorilla be true?
He follows men home just to cause strife
Between them and the wife.
It's enough to make a grown man sob,
If it's not the gorilla, it can only be the dog!

Geraldene Gillespie

NOT THE SAME

I'm not the same
Not like you
I can't do things
The others do

It's alright for them
Cos they're the same
Work to them
Is just a game.

It's hard for me
Because of my balance
Competing with them
Is quite a challenge.

So give me a chance
I'll do what I can
I can't do a lot
I'm a disabled man.

But there are things
That I can do
Because the Lord
Has seen me through.

Things may be
Difficult for me
But what I can't do now
I'll do in eternity.

D Mason

WELL, IF YOU MUST KNOW . . .

She thought him quite the charmer
As he crossed the dance floor, nifty
He had sideburns like a farmer
And a hint of something shifty
Hung about him like a dangerous cravat

There was no real need to worry though
For there was no real drama
And his frantic explanation
Made her feel just that bit calmer
'Ice cubes!
Spilled!
Upon the chair on which I sat!'

In shock, he stood up quickly
Trousers fraught with sudden terror
Melting ice unpleasant, trickly
Partygoers made the error
Of assuming it was all some kind of dance

So it was that he had reached her
But she saw the man inside
Both forgot about the ice cubes
For his trousers now had dried
And that is how your mother and I first met.

Rich Davenport

A Day To Remember

Sitting on the terrace in Madeira,
Overlooking a beautiful, picturesque bay,
The colours of the flowers so vibrant,
I knew it was to be a very special day.

Bougainvillaea and orchids, hibiscus,
Red and orange and purple galore,
Terracotta rooftops and palm trees,
There was great excitement in store.

And there in the distance we saw her,
She was mighty, the Queen Mary 2,
She glided into port in all her glory,
With a background so vividly blue.

A flotilla of ships all around her,
People lined up on the quay,
Children were singing and dancing,
She was such a wonder to see.

The cameras were snapping and flashing,
The artists were out by the score,
We walked down the hill to get closer,
And stopped for a drink near the shore.

Gazing on as the passengers disembarked,
It was a glorious day, the sun shone,
But by six, with a blast of her horn,
Disappearing into the sunset, she was gone.

June Melbourn

WATER
(Part of a collection of poems entitled The Element)

Happily splashing,
Swimming around
Then humbly swayed in the power displayed,
Smashing.
Realising my place in the scheme of all things,
While exposed to the mercy of elements the phone rings,
'I've carried this pad for a year and a day,
Jotting down insights I want to relay,
But nothing comes close to these gifts you display,
Like watching the sun rise from that hilltop today.'
Refreshed by exposure I want to move on,
Propelled by the truth but the search is still on,
Trying to submit my daft outfits dismissed,
Got to get my name written up on that list.

Benjamin Paul Smith

WE BLAME THE FRENCH!

We are descendants of Africans, English,
French and Portuguese.
Of all of these
We blame the French.
Do we blame them for making us a colony?
No, we blame them for our anger
and eccentricity.
From Africa, we get our nobility,
from the English our love of history.
We've made no claim on the Portuguese
but we blame the French with ease.
We looked at ourselves and thought,
which one of these nationalities
is responsible for our irrationality?
When we argue, fight and cuss
We blame the French in us!

Arlene Patricia Carr

MEANDERING

I loiter rural lanes nigh
Near river bank, hedgerows green
Placid waters flowing by
Sunlight glow enhancing beauty of sylvan scene

Reeds a-rustling in breeze
Birds nesting there
Splendour, wonder to perceive
Speckled feathers, movements everywhere

Pleasure mine spills over
Flora, meadowsweet white
Mountain, valley, grandeur
Beauty, charm in glow of sunlight

Clouds white, source of beauty
Float across sky blue
Sunlight paints buttercups, daisies
Images, adding zest to lifetime anew.

Ivy Lott

FEATHERED FRIENDS

Our garden is a real delight
With little birds touched down in flight.
The humble sparrow always comes
Grateful for those tasty crumbs.

I saw the woodpecker today
With his technicolour coat so gay.
How could there be no sovereign Lord
With such beauty to be adored?

Thrushes sing their tuneful song
Blue tits and chaffinches join the throng
Old friend robin is perched on the tree
With red breast resplendent for all to see.

They need no engines, coils or springs;
They soar above on feathery wings,
Enrapturing all who may pass by
These friendly monarchs of the sky.

Lyn Hunter

FEEDING THE SEAGULL

'Watch this,' my Uncle said
Holding out a piece of bread
As seagulls circled overhead.

'One of them will swoop down low,
And take the bread, gently, you know.'
But Uncle was wrong. It wasn't so.

The gull swooped in, it didn't linger
It took the bread - and Uncle's finger.

Susan Gordon

SATURDAY DAD!

Saturday Dad with his son for the day,
Holding him close in the tube train sway.
Tender lips just touching his hair
Almost afraid to show his care
Where do they go on this their day?
Too cold for the *beach* or a *park* to *play!*
A whole day with Dad, then back home to Mum.
A saddening sight, that's so often seen.
A couple apart -
A child torn between.

Cynthia Taylor

TAKE AS INSTRUCTED

A pill for this, a capsule for that,
do 'they' all know, what they're at?
Thousands of doctors, GPs galore,
billions of tablets; what are they for?

Every ache, symptom or pain,
all sorts of conditions, treated the same;
the same - by the mouth, is what I mean,
be it your heart, lungs, liver or spleen!

All coughs and all colds are treated alike,
at all waking hours and oft, thro' the night.
'Take two with water,' a meal or whatever;
throughout the years, and all kinds of weather!

We're a funny old lot - the human race,
and - as a species, a bit of a disgrace!
No other creatures seemingly suffer like we;
a fact - upon which, I hope all will agree?

So why do we lend ourselves to all sorts of things,
unlike huge elephants, whales or birds on the wing?
Why should *we* suffer these ailments and ills,
could it just be to make rich those who produce all these pills?

Peter Mahoney

DARK DAYS IN 1900

As the sun departs on this bleak frost-nipped day,
the toffs are OK.
Wandering back to a hot full plate
and a hearty fire in the grate.
It's no trouble.

But what is the fate of the empty pocketed boy?
His hunger is deep and cold like the snow.
And where will he sleep?
A master's barn beckons.
Will there be work tomorrow?

He clears deep snow in the biting wind,
Hands and feet numb too.
The copper received will buy that steaming soup,
but despair creeps in
at the hole in his shoe.

Mary E Wain

ANCHOR BOOKS
SUBMISSIONS INVITED
SOMETHING FOR EVERYONE

ANCHOR BOOKS GEN - Any subject,
light-hearted clean fun, nothing unprintable
please.

THE OPPOSITE SEX - Have your say on the
opposite gender. Do they drive you mad or can
we co-exist in harmony?

THE NATURAL WORLD - Are we destroying
the world around us? What should we do to
preserve the beauty and the future of our planet -
you decide!

All poems no longer than 30 lines.
Always welcome! No fee!
Plus cash prizes to be won!

Mark your envelope (eg *The Natural World)*
And send to:
Anchor Books
Remus House, Coltsfoot Drive
Peterborough, PE2 9JX

**OVER £10,000 IN POETRY PRIZES
TO BE WON!**

Send an SAE for details on our latest
competition!